Reps Vs Dems

Facts You Might Want To Know
(or not)

Unbiased Comparisons Of Which Political Party Is Really Better For You!!

Content

As an old codger with too much time on his hands, I have, over the last few years, become more and more cynical and distrusting of the synthetic rhetoric coming out of the mouths of politicians and their staunchest allies.

There is an old saying that says, "Figures don't lie, but liars figure." I am going to challenge that saying by using statistics such as dates, The Dow Jones Industrial Average, the years when Reps or Dems came into office, the archives of the US Government Agencies, (of which there are many,) and any other reputable source that can be easily verified by those in doubt.

Whenever possible, I would like to go back to the so-called Golden Years of the 1950's to start and include the current year of 2010 or as much of it as there is.

Confessing that I, like many of you, have in all probability some preconceived ideas of what is the truth, I am fully prepared to see the error of my ways. They say, "The truth shall set you free." We'll see. So lets get to it.

Let's see if most of us can agree that the health, or lack thereof, of our economy is EVENTUALLY reflected in the direction of stock prices. Now I know that some will not agree and try to spin it their way but over time it is true.

The Dow Jones Industrial Average, (hereinafter called the Dow) is a stock index that has been historically used to measure the market movement over time. When someone asks how the market did today, the answer is usually expressed in Dow points, which, by the way, are not dollars.

The question I asked myself was, how has the market fared under Rep administrations vs. Dem administrations ? Right now I don't know the answer, but I will, and soon.

Years	Party	Dow open	Dow close	Net points
1953-1960	republican	292	616	324
1961-1968	democrat	610	944	334
1969-1976	republican	948	1005	57
1977-1980	democrat	1000	964	-36
1981-1992	republican	973	3301	2328
1993-2000	democrat	3309	10788	7479
2001-2008	republican	10646	8776	-1870
2009-2010	democrat	9035	10584	1549
Total Rep. Dow points	839	Total Dem. Dow points	9326	

So, 9326 for the Dems And 839 for the Reps. Seems like quite a disparity. The numbers look a little better when you add the percentages for each party and divide by the number of years in office. The annual percentages than show the Dems at 13.905% and the Reps at 9.389%. A difference of 48%.

I don't think I've done anything unfair with these numbers, but there is another way to look at this. It may be doing a disservice to attribute credit or blame to either party for starting the time clock on economic conditions before the new administration has even been sworn in. With that thinking in mind, and considering that the public wants to see almost immediate change in his or her economic status, I thought it might be more fair not to charge the newcomers with the first six months results. Our economy is so huge that trying to turn it around quickly would be like turning an aircraft carrier on a dime. Not possible.

Years	Party	Dow open	Dow close	Net points
6/53-6/61	Republican	268	684	416
6/61-6/69	Democrat	684	873	189
6/69-6/77	Republican	873	916	43
6/77-6/81	Democrat	916	977	61
6/81-6/93	Republican	977	3516	2539
6/93-6/01	Democrat	3516	10502	6986
6/01-6/09	Republican	10502	8447	-2055
6/09-12/09	Democrat	8447	10584	2137

Total Rep. Points   943   Total Dem. Points   9373

So 9373 for the Dems. And 943 for the Reps., a little better for the Reps., but not much.

What is going on here? I was always under the impression that the Reps favored business while the Dems represented the working man.

Upon consulting with two people whose opinions I respect, I discovered that they both felt that political control of Congress might be an important factor in assigning credit or blame for an administrations statistical results. We now need to know which party controlled Congress and when. We also need to know if that Congress was of the same party as the administration in office or of the opposing party. This is starting to get a little complicated, but it could be enlightening. .

Years	President	Congress	Dow %
81-89	Rep	Dem	96.3
89-93	Rep	Dem	49.2
93-95	Dem	Dem	16.2
95-01	Dem	Rep	128
01-07	Rep	Rep	20.1
07-09	Rep	Dem	-29.6
09-10	Dem	Dem	15.4

If we add the Dow %'s for the years with Rep presidents and Dem congress and divide by the years involved, which was 14, we get 8.28%. Now we add for Dem presidents and Dem congress and divide by 3 we get 10.54%.

Now lets do the same for Dem presidents and Rep congress and we come up with 128 divided by 6 for a percentage of 21.33. Doing the same for Rep presidents and Rep congress we get 20.1 divided by 6 equals 3.35%.

So #1 is Dem presidents with Rep congress at 21.33%. #2 is Dem presidents with Dem congress at 10.54%. #3 is Rep presidents with Dem congress at 8.28%. And last place goes to Rep presidents with Rep congresses with 3.35%.

Quite obviously we are better off with a Democratic administration and a Republican congress as our historic system of checks and balances encourages cooperation.

Many of you may be thinking, "Well, there's more to life than just our economy and money. I couldn't agree more. This book, however, is about politics and facts, not theories and beliefs that many of us have accepted as truisms from an accepted seer. I know I was brought up listening to my father and how Harry Truman was leading us to "Rack and Ruin." It's also become evident to me that so many of us only watch and listen to what we want to believe that we become even more biased and prejudiced.

So what's another political belief that is important and can be measured fairly and objectively?

How about government spending and our national debt? Let's see if we can figure out this deal and act in a manner to avoid "Rack and Ruin."

Let's insert a table here and call it Federal Debt As A Percentage Of Gross Domestic Product. The reason the dates in the following table seem to be a bit weird is that our government budget year runs from the beginning of October to the end of September.

Year	Party	Percentage
10/53-9/61	Republican	62
10/61-9/69	Democrat	46
10/69-9/77	Republican	36
10/77-9/81	Democrat	33.5
10/81-9/89	Republican	45.4
10/89-9/93	Republican	61.7
10/93-9/01	Democrat	63.4
10/01-9/09	Republican	67.7

The Reps were in office for a total of 36 years. The Dems for 20 years. When you add the Reps percentages and divide by 36, you get 7.578 % per year. The Dems come to 7.145%. That's a difference of over 6% a year. Not a big difference, but it does add up. Apparently, over time, the Dems spend less as a percent of GDP.

To dig a little deeper into what's going on now, lets look at our slow emergence from this recent horrific recession. Most people acknowledge that we need faster job growth. Some of those same people are calling for an end to government stimulus programs.

You know what? You can't have both at the same time! Cutting government spending now will hasten more job loss and we will fall back into a double dip recession. The time to cut government spending is when payrolls are expanding.

Net monthly payroll change is reported by the Bureau of Labor Statistics and is an excellent predictor of our country's economic health. Let's see if the Reps or the Dems have a better track record at job creation. Let's add them up by year and political party and find out which party is better at stimulating job growth.

Dates	Party	Jobs gained or lost
1953-1960	Reps	4,160,000
1961-1968	Dems	15,502,000
1969-1976	Reps	11,264,000
1977-1980	Dems	11,129,000
1981-1992	Reps	18,526,000
1993-2000	Dems	23,291,000
2001-2008	Reps	2,589,000
2009 +	Dems	-4,183,000

Adding the totals show that the Reps were responsible for 36,539,000 jobs created over a period of 36 years and the Dems for 45,739,000 over a period of 21 years, both on a calendar year basis. To arrive at a fair comparison, divide the jobs by the years and the numbers show 1,014,972 jobs created per year by the Reps and 2,178,047 by the Dems. That's a difference in favor of the Dems by 1,163,075 jobs per year on average. The percentage difference is 114.59%. That's just huge.

Once again, if we look at the fairness of these numbers, it just seems that crediting jobs created to a newly elected administration for the first six months of their term isn't quite right as they had little impact on policy that created these job gains or losses.

When we adjust the job creation numbers to account for this, the new totals look like this.

Date	Party	Jobs gained or lost
6/53-6/61	Reps	4,036,000
6/61-6/69	Dems	16,659,000
6/69-6/77	Reps	11,913,000
6/77-6/81	Dems	9,635,000
6/81-6/93	Reps	19,228,000
6/93-6/01	Dems	21,621,000
6/01-6/09	Reps	-2,077,000
6/09-12/09	Dems	-824,000

Now when we divide by 36 and 20.5 respectfully, the numbers look like this. Reps had 33,100,000 divided by 36 equals 919,444 and the Dems had 47,091,000 divided by 20.5 equals 2,297,121 jobs created per year on average. The difference is even wider. It amounts to 1,377,677 per year for a percentage difference of 149.8%. WOW!!

Never in a million years would I have expected that. No comment necessary as it speaks for itself.

The huge differential in jobs created causes me to consider analyzing this by including congressional control as well as Presidential control. Let's start with Reagan's term and go from there.

Years	Presidents	Congress	Jobs
81-89	Rep	Dem	15,935,000
89-93	Rep	Dem	2,591,000
93-95	Dem	Dem	6,642,000
95-01	Dem	Rep	16,428,000
01-07	Rep	Rep	5,099,000
07-09	Rep	Dem	-1,926,000
09-10	Dem	Dem	-4,164,000

So, Rep Presidents and Dem congress created 16,600,000 jobs in 14 years, an average of 1,185,714 per year.

Rep Presidents and Rep congress created 5,099,000 jobs in 6 years, an average of 849,833 per year.

Dem Presidents and Dem congress created 2,478,000 in 3 years, an average of 826,000 per year.

Dem Presidents and Rep congress created 16,428,000 jobs in 6 years, an average of 2,738,000 per year.

Analyzing this without spin gives a big edge to Dem Presidents with Rep congress, followed by Rep Presidents with Dem congress, then by Rep Presidents with Rep congress, and last by Dem Presidents with Dem congress.

.

What else should we be concerned about? Many of you may be worried about inflation. That's certainly legitimate but first a word on an even bigger financial monster. Neither party wants to even use this word but it is deflation and it's what we are slowly and painfully emerging from. When the housing bubble broke, it became obvious that almost everything had to shrink. Home values shrank. Investment accounts shrank. Jobs shrank. That's what deflation is and it's wicked to recover from. Just ask the Japanese. Enough already about deflation.

Lets look at inflation that has to return, at least to some degree, as it's the way the government pays off debt! That's right, the government is now issuing debt to stimulate the economy with the knowledge that eventually inflation will cause the face value of those notes and bonds to sink, allowing us to buy them back cheaper. Such a deal! Anyway, lets see which party handles rampant inflation better, the Reps or the Dems. Remember, about 2 to 2.5% inflation is actually a good thing as it bails us out.

Year	Party	Average annual rate of inflation
1953-1960	Reps	1.365
1961-1968	Dems	2.055
1969-1976	Reps	6.376
1977-1980	Dems	9.73
1981-1992	Reps	4.56
1993-2000	Dems	2.596
2001-2008	Reps	2.837
2009	Dems	-.34

The Reps average annual rate of inflation came in at 4.205%, while the Dems totaled 6.686%. That is a very substantial difference in favor of the Reps. The percentage differential is 59%. Hopefully we've learned a lot about inflation since the 1970's and early 1980's.

To sum up the statistical analysis, it would appear that the Dems have a decided advantage overall.

I would like now to present some of my own thoughts, observations and ideas. Hopefully they will not be construed as biased or one-sided, but will be accepted at face value. One of the benefits of having this information in written form is the ability to stop reading and, if angered or upset, set this book aside or even throw it away. (don't damage your Kindle, simply delete it).

One of the area's that shall forever remain a mystery to me is how people vote based on their feelings, apparent popularity, or just plain old charisma of the competing candidates. Let's look at the Presidents elected going back to Eisenhower and compare the above attributes to their defeated opponents.

Eisenhower vs. Adlai Stevenson - 1952 and 1956. Ike was a war hero who had never previously held an elected office. The General had superb leadership skills and was the last non-political President we elected. The feeling was that Stevenson had no chance but someone had to run. The majority did indeed like Ike.

Kennedy vs. Nixon - 1960. Charisma and popularity personified, Kennedy had to overcome the then important fact that he was Catholic. Nixon's chances were hurt when he was made to look sickly during a national debate by having his make-up applied by a Kennedy supporter. Charisma wins again.

Johnson vs. Goldwater - 1964. Slick talking, large state liberal against small state arch conservative. Johnson had an advantage as the incumbent. Definitely more charismatic at the time but vilified later due to the totally false Gulf of Tonkin Resolution, which escalated the Vietnam war. This was a landslide victory that proved to be a bad choice.

Nixon vs. Herbert Humphrey - 1968. Both career politicians. Conservatism becoming increasingly popular and Nixon was the Conservative. The country was also tired of the Vietnam war.

Nixon vs. George McGovern - 1972. The conservative and the incumbent, a tough combination to beat. He got us out of Vietnam but the unnecessary Watergate scandal forced his resignation. Remember "I am not a crook"?

Carter vs. Gerald Ford - 1976. Supposedly the sharp southern liberal vs. the likeable conservative, Carter criticized Fords handling of inflation and later proved inept at handling inflation himself. Not the best choice.

Reagan vs. Carter - 1980. Super charismatic, immensely popular, a conservative. What more could we ask for. Broke the back of inflation thru Paul Volker, intimidated the "evil empire", and stimulated the economy by deficit spending. Carter had no chance.

Reagan vs. Mondale -1984. No chance for Mondale either. Reagan's big mistake was not reeling in that deficit spending that was needed four years prior but not appropriate during growth years.

Bush Sr. vs. Dukakis - 1988. Rode in on the coattails of the still popular Reagan. Continued hiking deficit spending during expansionary times. Not good.

Clinton vs. Bush Sr. - 1992. Another personable and charismatic choice. Vilified by many over a sex scandal, Clinton started paying down the national debt.

Clinton vs. Dole - 1996. The national debt count-down clock slowed, then stopped, and then reversed! How soon we forget the good stuff to concentrate on the sensational. Clinton also had low unemployment, low inflation, and reduced welfare rolls.

Bush Jr. vs. Gore - 2000.
Bush Jr. vs. Kerry -2004.
I was taught that if you don't have anything good to say about a person, don't say anything at all.

Obama vs. McCain - 2008
Too early. What a thankless job, dragging us out of this mess.

The problem as I see it, is that when someone says "I'm a Democrat." or, "I'm a Republican.", they are subliminally tagged with the Liberal or Conservative mantels respectively.

In all likelihood, the Democrat does not want regulations strengthened to the point of restricting business and decreasing freedoms. The Republican does not want regulations eased to the point of legalized stealing and letting people do anything they want.

The Democrat does not want to pay more taxes. The Republican does not want a tax cut that would harm our freedoms.

I could go on and on with this but it probably would get as ridiculous as branding all Democrats as ultra- liberal and all Republicans as arch- conservatives. I think the vast majority of Democrats would like to have seen Bush be more successful. I think the vast majority of Republicans do not want Obama to fail as at least one infamous person has said.

Why not start a NEW political party, leaving all the hard core and idealist factions twisting in the wind. A new party that embraces the spirit and cooperation that has made us the strong and envied country that we used to be?

Call us the American Party, or the All American Party, or the American Cooperative Party and stop this ridiculous charade that power, prestige, and possessions are what we want when we all know that in the long run they are worthless and will continue to degrade our way of life.

GO USA!!

What should be done now to insure the financial crisis won't be repeated?

The Glass-Steagall act of 1933 worked well for over sixty years. REINSTATE IT!

Disallow securitization of mortgages!

Reinstate the net capital ratio back to the twelve to one ratio that existed prior to April, 28th, 2004!

www.ingramcontent.com/pod-product-compliance
Lightning Source LLC
Chambersburg PA
CDIIW072012280526

45788CB00005B/2021